S0-ART-983

From Dad for
Mother's Day 2004

WHY IT PAYS TO BE A
CHRISTIAN

All Scripture quotations in this book are taken from the King James Version of the Bible unless otherwise noted.

Why It Pays To Be A Christian

Copyright ©2003 by Midnight Call Ministries
Published by The Olive Press, a subsidiary of Midnight Call, Inc.
Columbia, South Carolina, 29228

Copy Editor: Susanna Cancassi
Proofreaders: Angie Peters, Susanna Cancassi
Layout/Design: Michelle Kim
Lithography: Simon Froese
Cover Design: Michelle Kim

Library of Congress Cataloging-in-Publication Data

Lieth, Norbert
        Why It Pays To Be A Christian
        ISBN #0-937422-57-6

        1. Biblical Teaching
        2. Counseling
        3. Evangelism
        4. Discipleship

All rights reserved. No portion of this book may be reproduced in any form without the written permission of the publisher.

Printed in the United States of America

The sole purpose of publishing this book is to
encourage the reader to surrender and consecrate
his life to Jesus Christ.

All funds received from the sale of this book will be
used exclusively to further the Gospel.

No one associated with this ministry receives a
royalty for any of the literature published by
The Olive Press.

$\mathscr{C}$ONTENTS

ಐ

Introduction

*W*hat is Christianity? What is being a true Christian worth today? Voltaire was a confirmed atheist. King Friedrich the Great of Germany met with Voltaire, and when he raised his glass, he said mockingly, "I will give my place in heaven for a Prussian mark." Silence filled the room until another guest in King Friedrich's court turned to Voltaire and said, "My lord, we have a law in Prussia, according to which everyone who wishes to sell something must first produce evidence that the object actually belongs to him. Can you prove that you have a place in heaven?"

VOLTAIRE

That is precisely the subject we will be dealing with in this book: heaven. The Bible teaches that the prerequisite for heaven is a genuine relationship with Jesus Christ. This relationship is the result of our putting faith in Him.

According to God's Word, those of us who are born again have the confirmation and testimony of the Holy Spirit in our hearts so that we can say, "Yes, I am saved." Such an admission is not prideful; it is humble, because we no longer rely on ourselves and our works, but on Jesus Christ alone. We have recognized that we are sinners and that we cannot be saved by doing good works or anything else. This is why we come to Jesus, asking Him to save us. The Lord hears this type of prayer. As a result, the Holy Spirit puts the testimony in our hearts that we are saved and belong to Jesus.

Jesus: Unique, Incomparable And Wonderful

Jesus cannot be compared with anything or anyone. He is the Christ, the Son of the Living God, and that is why it is worth being a Christian! The Song of Solomon proclaims that Jesus is indeed incomparable and wonderful: "What is thy beloved more than another beloved, O thou fairest among women? What is thy beloved more than another beloved, that thou dost so charge us? My beloved is white and ruddy, the chiefest among ten thousand. His head is as the most fine gold, his locks are bushy, and black as a raven. His eyes are as the eyes of doves by the rivers of water, washed with milk, and fitly set. His cheeks are as a bed of spices, as sweet flowers: his lips like lilies, dropping sweet smelling myrrh. His hands are as gold rings set with beryl: his belly is as bright ivory overlaid with sapphires. His legs are as pillars of marble, set upon sockets of fine gold: his countenance is as Lebanon, excellent as the cedars. His mouth is most sweet: yea, he is altogether lovely. This is my beloved, and this is my friend, O daughters of Jerusalem" (Song of Solomon 5:9–16).

Chapter 1

Jésus: Unique, Incomparable and Wonderful in His Testimony

*J*ohn's Gospel account contains a number of Christ's personal testimonies. For instance, He said:

- "I am the bread of life: he that cometh to me shall never hunger; and he that believeth on me shall never thirst" (John 6:45).

- "I am the light of the world: he that followeth me shall not walk in darkness, but shall have the light of life" (John 8:12).

- "I am the door: by me if any man enter in, he shall be saved, and shall go in and out, and find pasture" (John 10:9).

- "I am the good shepherd: the good shepherd giveth his life for the sheep" (John 10:11).

- "I am the resurrection, and the life: he that believeth in me, though he were dead, yet shall he live" (John 11:25).

- "I am the way, the truth, and the life: no man cometh unto the Father, but by me" (John 14:6).

"I am the true vine, and my Father is the husbandman" (John 15:1).

- "I am the true vine, and my Father is the husbandman" (John 15:1).

When the Samaritan woman told Jesus, "I know that Messiah cometh, which is called Christ: when he is come, he will tell us all things," He replied, "I that speak unto thee am he" (John 4:25–26).

To Pilate's question, "Art thou a king then?" Jesus answered, "Thou sayest that I am a king. To this end was I born, and for this cause came I into the world, that I should bear witness unto the truth. Every one that is of the truth heareth my voice" (John 18:37).

The disciples heard Jesus' testimonies and they also saw His works.

Let's assume that we are standing before some of the first Christians and are able to ask them why they are believers. The following conversations might take place.

Peter

"Peter, why are you a Christian? You were a man who knew how to assert yourself. You had an occupation, a livelihood. You were happily married, and apparently you also had a good mother-in-law. You were a leader; a true Israelite who had both feet firmly planted on the ground. You knew what you wanted. You did not waste your time when it came to drawing your sword. In one sentence, can you please explain why you became a Christian?"

Peter: "I can tell you why in very few words: 'We believe and are sure that thou art that Christ, the Son of the living God' (John 6:69). 'Thou art the Christ, the Son of the living God' (Matthew 16:16). In other words, the other apostles and I lived with Him, heard Him, and got to know Him because we were with Him almost daily for three years. That is why I am quite certain that Jesus is indeed the promised Christ. And that is why I, a Jew, have come to believe in Jesus."

Paul

"Paul, why did you become a Christian? You were a Pharisee who strictly obeyed and enforced the law. You were an educated man, but you hated Jesus and His Church, and you persecuted them to the point of death. You tried to force Jesus' disciples to deny His name. Why have things changed so radically?"

Paul: "I became a disciple of Jesus because something completely extraordinary happened to me as I was travelling to Damascus to persecute the Christians there, 'I saw in the way a light from heaven, above the brightness of the sun, shining round about me and them which journeyed with me. And when we were all fallen to the earth, I heard a voice speaking unto me, and saying in the Hebrew tongue, Saul, Saul, why persecutest thou me? It is hard for thee to kick against the pricks. And I said, Who art thou, Lord? And he said, I am Jesus whom thou persecutest'" (Acts 26:13– 15).

"Apparently this was a great turning point in your life. But Paul, what do you think today? Before your experience on the road to Damascus, you tried to suppress faith in Jesus. As an educated Pharisee, you could surely have had a brilliant career."

Paul: " 'Yea doubtless, and I count all things but loss for the excellency of the knowledge of Christ

Jesus my Lord: for whom I have suffered the loss of all things and do count them but dung, that I may win Christ' (Philippians 3:8). 'None of these things move me, neither count I my life dear unto myself, so that I might finish my course with joy, and the ministry, which I have received of the Lord Jesus, to testify the gospel of the grace of God'"(Acts 20:24).

John

"John, why did you and your brother, James, become Christians and leave your father's boat, your livelihood and your career? You were 'he-men' and were even known as the 'sons of thunder'! It might easily have been said about you two, 'Better not upset them!' But now you, John, are called the 'apostle of love.' Will you explain that, please?"

John: "Certainly. 'That which was from the beginning, which we have heard, which we have seen with our eyes, which we have looked upon, and our hands have handled, of the Word of life; (For the life was manifested, and we have seen it, and bear witness, and shew unto you that eternal life, which was with the Father, and was manifested unto us'" (1st John 1:1–2).

"So you still maintain today that the life of Jesus and the life that He gives are eternal?"

John: "Yes. 'That which we have seen and heard declare we unto you, that ye also may have fellowship with us: and truly our fellowship is with the Father, and with his Son Jesus Christ'" (1st John 1:3).

John, why did you and your brother, James, become Christians and leave your father's boat, your livelihood and your career?

"John, do you know what you're saying? Do you know that these statements put Jesus Christ above all men who have ever lived?"

John: "Yes, 'And the Word was made flesh, and dwelt among us, (and we beheld his glory, the glory as of the only begotten of the Father,) full of grace and truth'" (John 1:14).

"But John, you're saying that we see the Father in Jesus. Obviously you must be referring to the tabernacle. There the glory of God was revealed, and now you are claiming that Jesus *is* this glory! Don't let the Israelites hear that…!"

John: "I know exactly what I am saying, for, 'No man hath seen God at any time; the only begotten Son, which is in the bosom of the Father, he hath declared him'" (John 1:18).

"John, please allow me to quote from a Bible commentary on the words, 'For the Jews there was nothing greater than the law. For all men, there is no greater desire than to see God. Here is more than the law. Here is the fulfilment of all desire.

21

Through Jesus, who is completely one with the Father, and concentrated on Him with His whole being, we learn all that is essential about God. Through Him come both grace and truth in one.' You would surely agree with this."

The Samaritans In Sychar

The Samaritans in Sychar were men, women and children. Our question to them is, "Why did you become Christians? You didn't let yourselves be talked into it by a woman, did you?"

Samaritans: "No, we didn't, and we told the woman this quite clearly: 'Now we believe, not because of thy saying: for we have heard him ourselves, and know that this is indeed the Christ, the Saviour of the world'" (John 4:42).

The Centurion At The Cross

"You saw many people die on a cross, and probably even ordered Jesus' crucifixion. The Roman emperor was your god, to whom you were completely devoted. Your occupation, your wages, your future and your life were at stake. I assume that your position as a centurion demanded maturity and caution; you had experience in battle..."

Centurion: "Yes, I was used to seeing many things. I knew many people; among them, heroic soldiers and admirable, noble officers. I saw many people die, experienced their final hours and heard them weep, curse and lament. But no one died like Jesus. I could come to no other conclusion than this; 'Truly, this man was the Son of God'" (Mark 15:39).

Present-Day People

Today, people also testify how they came to know Jesus Christ, and what effect this decision has on their lives:

" I did not hear much about true Christianity when I was younger. I studied theology and became a minister, but I was a pastor without Jesus for a long time. I concerned myself with many social issues, and I tried to help where I saw a need, but only now do I know that I was lacking the decisive experience. Now Jesus has become my Lord. I have found Him, or, rather, He has found me! Now I am carrying out my ministry as a pastor in a completely different way. I try to tell people about Jesus and lead them to Him. My interest in all other issues is not less, but deeper. My main task, however, is to help build the Church of Jesus Christ, and make a real contribution to solving the many other issues.

ॺ

66 I was unfaithful to my wife for 23 years, but she loves me more than ever, even though I am in prison at the moment. I wanted to end my life during the first days of my imprisonment. But it all turned out quite differently. The Lord didn t allow it to happen, and I came to a living faith in God the Lord. I immediately wrote my wife and asked her to send me a Bible. She did so and wrote me, This is our wedding Bible; I need the other one myself. I have never cried so much in my life as when I read our wedding Bible for the first time! And I had to go to prison to do this. Because I had no time, as the title of the tract that was given to me, says. Now I know that the most important thing in life is to follow Jesus!

ৱ

"It has been more than 40 years since I realized that I had sinned against God and man, and that these sins separated me from God because He has to judge sin. It became clear to me that this judgment would mean eternal damnation. But simultaneously I heard the Good News of salvation: Whoever confesses his sins to the Lord and asks Jesus Christ for forgiveness in faith experi-

"...when I grieved the Lord and was unhappy, but Jesus was always the same good and faithful Shepherd. He cared for His child."

ences forgiveness and receives eternal life. God s wonderful offer overwhelmed me and I accepted it with a grateful heart. Looking back, I can only rejoice with thanks and amazement! I went through highs and lows which included my faith life when I grieved the Lord and was unhappy, but Jesus was always the same good and faithful Shepherd. He cared for His child. Only those who have experienced it can know what it means to have the deep assurance and practical experience that He will never leave His own or come too late in difficulties and distress. I have never regretted my decision to surrender my heart and life to Jesus. On the contrary, I cannot understand how some-one can live without Jesus in today s world, where all values are questioned and wickedness is increasing. According to Scripture, it is not only the present that is at stake, but also the future, which must be unimaginably wonderful.

"I was baptized and raised as a Roman Catholic. By the grace of God I found Jesus and received Him as my Savior and Redeemer. I was also able to find a home church that I have come to love. The Word of God has become more and more important to me. The Bible has become my favorite book. I want to understand the Word of God and live a life that is pleasing to the Lord.

ॐ

"I was at one of your meetings with a patient of mine, who does not own a car, who asked to be taken there. At the end of your message you challenged us to believe in and surrender our lives to Jesus. It was clear that this applied to me, and so I responded. Yes, Jesus called me on that day, and I am full of joy and gratitude. My profession as a physician demands a lot of strength but I now know that God gives me this strength anew every day. He also knows what He can ask of me. Right now I have two weeks of vacation so that I can leisurely contemplate the many beautiful things in His creation. When I talk with Him, I ask Him to allow me to continue my life in love and compassion for the people who entrust themselves to me.

ঽ

These testimonies agree with the statement someone made regarding Philippians 2:9, "Wherefore God also hath highly exalted him, and given him a name which is above every name. For many people, Jesus is merely a figure who is suitable for a painting, the main character in a heroic novel, a beautiful figure for a statue or the theme for a song. But to those who have heard His voice, experienced His forgiveness and felt His blessings, He is warmth, light, joy, hope and salvation, a Friend who never leaves us cast down, who picks us up when others push us down."

Chapter 2

Jésus: Unique, Incomparable and Wonderful in His Personality

His Greatness

The *Encyclopedia Britannica* uses 20,000 words to describe Jesus. This description takes up more space than the encyclopedia

ROUSSEAU

devotes to Aristotle, Cicero, Alexander the Great, Julius Caesar, Buddha, Confucius, Mohammed and Napoleon.

The following statements are from well-known people concerning Jesus:

NAPOLEON

French philosopher Jean-Jacques Rousseau said: "It would have been a greater miracle to invent such a life as that of Christ than His actual existence is."

At the end of his life, Napoleon Bonaparte, who engaged half of Europe in war, wrote these words in his diary: "With all my armies and generals, I have not been able to make one single continent subject to me in a quarter of a century. But this

Jesus has conquered nations and cultures without the use of arms for centuries."

Well-known historian H.G. Wells was asked what person had the greatest influence on history. He answered that if one were to judge the greatness of a man according to historical aspects, Jesus would be at the top of the list.

RENAN

Historian Kenneth Scott Latourette said, "The more time that passes, the more apparent it becomes that Jesus, measured by His influence on history, led the most momentous life that was ever lived on this planet. And His influence seems to increase."

Ernest Renan made the following observation, "Jesus is the most genial figure that ever lived in the historical field. His brilliance is eternal and His government will never cease. He is unique in every way and comparable with nothing and nobody. Without Christ history cannot be understood."

The Bible teaches that Jesus Christ is greater than all. His greatness is revealed in several passages in the epistle to the Hebrews:

• Jesus is greater than all of the angels (Hebrews 1:1 – 3:19).

• Jesus is greater than the high priesthood of Aaron (Hebrews 4:1 – 6:20).

• Jesus is greater than all of the revelations of salvation in the Old Testament (Hebrews 7:1 – 8:13).

• Jesus is greater than all the Old Testament sanctuaries and sacrifices (Hebrews 9:1 – 10:18, and 10:39).

• Jesus is the Author and Finisher of our faith (Hebrews 11:1 – 13:25).

His Sinlessness

Although Jesus taught His disciples the Lord's prayer, He never prayed it because He did not need to ask the Father to forgive Him of His trespasses

The thief on the cross said, "This man hath done nothing amiss" (Luke 23:41).

because He was without guilt, without sin and completely pure. He never had to regret anything. He never had to repent because He never sinned; therefore, He did not need to ask for forgiveness. He humbled Himself for others. He took our sins upon Himself and prayed, "Father, forgive them; for they know not what they do." Jesus was sinless; therefore, He was also holy and righteous.

• Pilate's wife sent a message to her husband, saying, "Have thou nothing to do with that just man"(Matthew 27:19).

35

- Pilate said, "I...have found no fault in this man" (Luke 23:14).
- The thief on the cross stated, "This man hath done nothing amiss" (Luke 23:41).
- The centurion at the cross exclaimed, "Certainly this was a righteous man" (Luke 23:47).
- Even the demons confessed, "Thou art the Holy One of God" (Mark 1:12).

Jesus Christ was sinless in contrast to all other men and founders of religions who ever lived. When He challenged a crowd, "Which of you convinceth me of sin?" (John 8:46), He received silence as a response. Romans 8:3 says, "For what the law could not do, in that it was weak through the flesh, God sending his own Son in the likeness of sinful flesh, and for sin, condemned sin in the flesh." The New International Version translates this as, "For what the law was powerless to do in that it was weakened by the sinful nature, God did by sending his own Son in the likeness of sinful man to be a sin offering. And so he condemned sin in sinful man" (see also 1st Peter 2:22 and Hebrews 4:15).

His Deity

French doctor and scientist Louis Pasteur said, "It is in the name of science that I proclaim Jesus Christ as the Son of God. My scientific mind, which attaches great value to the relationship between cause and effect, obliges me to acknowledge this. My need to worship finds in Him its complete satisfaction."

Many Old and New Testament verses testify that Jesus Christ is the Son of God. The Bible portrays Jesus as completely human (but without sin) and completely divine (compare, for instance, Isaiah 9:5–6; John 1:1–2; 3:16; 8:58; Philippians 2:6–7; Colossians 1:15–19; 1st Timothy 3:16; Hebrews 13:8; 1st John 5:20, etc).

Colossians 1:19–20 says, "For it pleased the Father that in him should all fullness dwell; and, having made peace through the blood of his cross, by him to reconcile all things unto himself; by him to reconcile all things unto himself; by him, I say, whether they be things in earth, or things in heaven." We can only worship Him in amazement with the words of Isaiah 46:5, "To whom will ye liken me, and make me equal, and compare me...?"

If you, my dear reader, accept the Bible's testimony concerning Jesus and if you acknowledge His unique nature, don't you think that the most sensible thing for you to do is to decide upon having a life with Him? If Jesus is all that which He maintained of Himself, then that is reason enough to become a Christian! If you have not done so already, surrender your life to Him and follow in His footsteps. If Jesus is that which He says of Himself, if He is that which the Bible says of

Him, and what people have experienced with Him, then *everyone* needs Him. Only through Him we receive forgiveness of our sins and to enter into the kingdom of heaven. With Him we win all; without Him we lose everything.

Shakespeare's Hamlet said, "I lose, whether I live or die." The Apostle Paul knew with all certainty, though, "I win, whether I live or die." You need to become a Christian, for without Jesus you will lose everything!

Friedrich Nietzsche is called the great philosopher of godlessness. As a 16-year old, he wrote of Jesus, "I know that if I don't find Him I will find no answer to my life." At the end of his life, in which he rejected Jesus, he wrote, "Woe betide those who have no homeland!"

In his play, "The Physicist," Swiss dramatist Friedrich Durrenmatt confessed, "When I no longer feared Him, my wisdom destroyed my riches." Those who have Jesus, however, are rich. "Ye are enriched by him" (1st Corinthians 1:5).

Chapter 3

Jésus: Unique, Incomparable and Wonderful in His Love

*F*irst John 3:16 says this about Jesus Christ: "Hereby perceive we the love of God, because he laid down his life for us..." Jesus' death on Calvary's cross is the proclamation of the eternal, unchanging and unfathomable love God has for a lost world, and therewith for every individual person. The shed blood of Christ is the proof of God's love for those who are burdened with sin and are far from Him: "But God commendeth his love toward us, in that, while we were yet sinners, Christ died for us" (Romans 5:8).

As the Son of God, Jesus was the only One who could die for the sins of man. He did this, and He did it for you! We fail to find this type of love in any other religion. Why? Because the Lord is love in Himself. Love is an attribute of His being. He cannot separate Himself from His love. This love began with God, who has no beginning or end. Somebody once said: "God is what He is, primarily on account of His love." And Friedrich Bodelschwingh coined the phrase, "There is no person on this earth that God does not love." God

Himself said, "I have loved thee with an everlasting love" in Jeremiah 31:3. Therefore, there is not one single person on this earth who is not loved by God.

God loves every person the same. He will never love one person more and another one less. Saint Augustine so beautifully explained that, "God loves every one of us as though there was nobody but us He could give His love to."

Nobody will ever be able to stand before God and maintain that he was not loved by Him. I am deeply con-

"What man of you, having an hundred sheep, if he lose one of them, doth not leave the ninety and nine in the wilderness, and go after that which is lost, until he find it?..."

vinced that when the lost appear before the throne of God, they will become horrified that they did not receive His love. If there were only one sinner on this earth, God, in His infinite love, would have done just as much for his/her salvation as He did in Jesus for the entire world.

This is exactly the point Jesus was trying to make in the parable of the lost sheep:

"What man of you, having an hundred sheep, if he lose one of them, doth not leave the ninety and nine in the wilderness, and go after that which is lost, until he find it? And when he hath found it, he layeth it on his shoulders, rejoicing. And when he cometh home, he calleth together his friends and neighbours, saying unto them, Rejoice with me; for I have found my sheep which was lost. I say unto you, that likewise joy shall be in heaven over one sinner that repenteth, more than over ninety and nine just persons, which need no repentance" (Luke 15:4–7).

Martin Luther described God's love with these words: "God is a glowing oven of love which reaches from heaven to earth."

Chapter 4

Jesus: Unique, Incomparable and Wonderful in His Forgiveness

hat We Need To Know About Sin

Sin means missing the mark. Sin can be defined as everything that does not correspond with God's nature: every act, every tendency, and every condition. The human race became corrupt through Adam's act of disobedience. Man's original perfection was completely destroyed. We only need to look around us to see how the world has degenerated.

Sin has destroyed all social order in mankind and this has affected marriages, families, societies and nations; it has caused infidelity, lies, hatred, war and death. Instead of working together, we now work against one another. Enmity, strife and war are everywhere. The Bible teaches that man's nature is so corrupt that he cannot produce anything good (Romans 3:10-12).

Furthermore, the Bible teaches that man is corrupt in his will (Romans 1:28), in his mind (2nd Corinthians 4:4), and in his conscience (1st

Every single sin that we commit, whether in thought, word or deed, is reckoned as sin by God.

Timothy 4:2), and that he is blinded in his heart (Jeremiah 17:9) and understanding (Ephesians 4:18; 2nd Corinthians 4:3-4). We are so completely corrupt that we do not become sinners through the sins that we commit, but we sin because we are sinners by nature. Every single sin that we commit, whether in thought, word or deed, is reckoned as sin by God.

And just as coal cannot be made white by washing it, neither can man be liberated from sin through his own efforts.

Seen in this light, we can better understand that there can only be one justification for man: not his own, but only that which comes through Jesus Christ, the Righteous One, of whom it is written: "...though your sins be as scarlet, they shall be as white as snow; though they be red like crimson, they shall be as wool"(Isaiah 1:18). Forgiveness through Jesus Christ is truly unique, incomparable and wonderful!

Former East Prussian president August Winning said, "I made a wide circle to avoid Christ, but I gradually came nearer to Him. I saw that man was evil through and through, and recognized that there was no exception. Not every man is a criminal, but every man has thoughts, wishes and lusts which weigh the same as murder. It is completely unthinkable that we can return to God from such rejection unless something takes place in us before. I understand that God has to condemn me for my sins, but I see His love, of which life testifies, and believe that He does not want to condemn, but extends His hand toward us. This hand of God is Christ."

I once read an article entitled, "Who is like Jesus?" The article said, "We can never tire Him; we cast all our cares and worries upon Him. He is always prepared to help us up; He always speaks to us with the same love and listens to what we have to say. There is no greater name than the name of Jesus. It is more glorious than the name of Caesar, more melodious than the name of Beethoven, more victorious than the name of Napoleon, more eloquent than that of Demosthenes, more patient than that of Lincoln.

The name of Jesus means life and love. The name of Jesus is like a glorious perfume. Who can sympathize with a homeless orphan like Jesus? Who can welcome home a lost son like Jesus? Who can liberate an alcoholic like Jesus? Who can fill a cemetery full of graves with the light of hope like Jesus? Who can make a woman on the street into a queen for God like Jesus? Who can gather the tears of human suffering like Jesus? Who can comfort us in our sorrows like Jesus?"

Many people try to correct their bad deeds through good works, but this does not help them. Others attempt to purify their souls through religious practices. That also fails. Others commit suicide as a result of a desperate conscience. But death does not free them because the soul lives on.

50

Only Jesus Christ, the Son of Man, has pow
earth to forgive sins (Matthew 9:6). Because He —
as the Son of God, as the just and sinless One, who
was not born of the seed of Adam but became man
through the Holy Spirit — can take upon Himself
all of the sins of all mankind. Just as through the
first Adam all men became sinners and were born
in sin, so all who believe on Jesus, the "last
Adam," are justified before God (Romans 5; 1st
Corinthians 15:45-48). In Adam, our sins are
reckoned unto us; in Jesus they are forgiven. Jesus
prepared the way for us into the Kingdom of God.

Peter triumphantly called out to the Jewish
authorities, "Him hath God exalted with his right
hand to be a Prince and a Saviour, for to give
repentance to Israel, and forgiveness of sins"
(Acts 5:31). Acts 10:43 says, "To him give all the
prophets witness, that through his name whoso-
ever believeth in him shall receive remission
of sins."

Micah was one of these prophets. He reverently exclaimed, "Who is a God like unto thee, that pardoneth iniquity, and passeth by the transgression of the remnant of his heritage? He retaineth not his anger for ever, because he delighteth in mercy" (Micah 7:18). Whoever surrenders to the Lord experiences the complete mercy of His forgiveness.

Jesus, You Are Different!

You stood beside the woman caught in adultery,
When all others kept their distance.
You visited the publican,
When all others were indignant.
You called the children to Yourself,
When all others wanted to send them away.
You forgave Peter,
When he condemned himself.
You praised the widow with her mite,
When nobody else noticed her.
You put the devil to flight,

When all others were deceived by him.
You promised the kingdom of heaven to the thief
on the cross,
When all others told him to go to hell.
You called Paul to follow you,
When all others feared him as a persecutor.
You fled fame,
When they all wanted to make You king.
You loved the poor,
When all others sought after riches.
You healed the sick,
When they were given up by others.
You were silent,
When they accused You, mocked You and
flogged You.
You died on the cross,
When they celebrated the Passover.
You took the blame upon Yourself,
When they washed their hands in innocence.
You rose from the dead,

When they thought it was all over.
Jesus, I thank You that You are!

— (Author unknown)

Chapter 5

Jésus: Unique, Incomparable and Wonderful in His Word

Historian Philip Schaff wrote this about Jesus: "He spoke words of life, as they had never been spoken before and were never spoken after Him. He achieved more than any other speaker or writer, without ever writing a single line Himself. He set more pens in motion and provided more material for sermons, speeches, discussions, textbooks, works of art and praise than the whole army of great men in ancient and modern times."

And someone else said of Jesus' words, "They are the words of a perfect man which, after they had been uttered, never died. On the contrary, the sound becomes louder. The echo of His words still moves hearts today. His Gospel is described as the power of God in Romans 1:16. Jesus Himself never spoke an empty word. With Him every single word has the weight of a rock; it gets to the bottom of things, breaks them apart and produces an echo."

Jewish author, Sholemash, admitted, "Jesus Christ is the excelling personality of all times.

Every action and every word of Jesus have value for all of us..."

Jesus Himself prophesied that His Gospel would be carried to the ends of the earth, which is taking place today (Matthew 24:14).

At the end of his life, Napoleon Bonaparte confessed, "I am dying before my time and my body will be returned to the earth to become the food of worms. This is the imminent fate of my greatness. What a difference between my deep misery and the eternal kingdom of Christ which is preached, loved, praised and spread over the whole earth."

Jesus promised that not even the gates of hell would be able to overcome His Church (Matthew 16:18). Kingdoms, power blocs and empires have come and gone. Many were hostile towards Christians, but they could not exterminate Christianity; on the contrary, it has grown. Jesus predicted the destruction of Jerusalem and the dispersion of the Jews amongst the nations, but He also predicted their restoration before His return (Luke 21:24). Our generation is witness to a newly restored Jewish state.

Jesus also predicted that the national identity of the Jewish people would be restored despite the centuries of Israel's dispersion (Jeremiah 31:36 and Matthew 24:34).

A man named Joachim Langhammer wrote, "Israel is a living miracle. It is a people which was hated and warred against for 4,000 years, and yet she could not be destroyed. On the contrary, there is no people on earth who are so much at the center of world history right now as the people of Israel!"

Jesus said, "Heaven and earth shall pass away: but my words shall not pass away"(Mark 13:31). His Word is like a rock in a storm; thousands of years of enmity towards it could not change it.

A Bible commentary says this about Jesus' words recorded in Mark 13:31: "If these words are not

"Israel is a living miracle. It is a people which was hated and warred against for 4,000 years, and yet she could not be destroyed."

true, then the man who made the statement is neither good nor holy but one of the greatest fools in the world. If they are true, however, then Jesus is all that He claimed to be: Creator, Lord of all times, Son of God and therewith God Himself. He surveyed a universe of radiant suns and circling galaxies and said that all this would pass away. In contrast to the dying suns and exploding stars, His words would never pass away. How can a worm such as man evade such statements?"

Engineer and geologist Baron von der Ropp, wrote, "The words of Jesus, 'all power is given unto me in heaven and on earth' caused me to study the whole of world history. It is striking that Christ is by far the most influential person in it. My studies ended with the recognition that old and new times really do find their meaning in Him, that only He has the key to the vision of history, that without Him it has no recognizable meaning."

But Jesus is also the fulfillment of nearly every Old Testament prophecy referring to the Messiah. More than 1,500 years before He came to this earth, it was prophesied...

• That he would come from the tribe of Judah (Genesis 49:10);

• That He would be of the house of David (Isaiah 11:1 and Jeremiah 33:21);

• That He would be born of a virgin (Isaiah 7:14);

• That He would come into the world in a little village called Bethlehem (Micah 5:1–2);

• That He would die a sacrificial death (Isaiah 53:1–12);

• That He would lose His life through crucifixion (Psalm 22:1–21);

• That He would rise from the dead (Psalm 16:8–11 and Isaiah 53:10–12);

• That He would return to the earth (Zechariah 14:4); and

• That He would appear in the clouds of heaven (Daniel 7:13).

Such predictions are vainly sought with regard to any other men or religions. There aren't any predictions regarding the coming of the prophet Mohammed, Buddha or any one else. These prophecies could only refer to one person. and that is Jesus Christ. Most prophecies have been fulfilled, and the ones that are not will also be fulfilled in Jesus, the man from Nazareth, the Son of the Living God!

No other person in world history can make this claim. And this unique, incomparable and wonderful Lord is calling you, dear reader, with a promise: "Him that cometh to me I will in no wise cast out" (John 6:37). Where will you go, if not to Him?

Chapter 6

Jésus: Unique,
Incomparable and
Wonderful in What He
Does with and for
His Own

To avoid any misunderstandings, or even self-deception, we must first ask, "Who are His own?" The risen Lord said,

- "Behold, I stand at the door, and knock: if any man hear my voice, and open the door, I will come in to him, and will sup with him, and he with me" (Revelation 3:20).

- "But as many as received him, to them gave he power to become the sons of God, even to them that believe on his name" (John 1:12).

- "He that hath the Son hath life; and he that hath not the Son of God hath not life" (1st John 5:12).

Those who make a conscious decision to receive Jesus into their hearts and lives belong to Him. He is their instructor, they are His own. Such a person is a child of God. Are you His child? If not, you must make this decision today, because every day without Him is a day wasted. Those who belong to Jesus will experience Him in their daily lives. They not only have a glorious hope for the future, but a present that contains immeasurable riches.

Tremendous things take place in your life when you make a decision for the Lord:

• Your relationship with God is no longer that of a sinner to a righteous judge, but the relationship of a child to a father: "Behold, what manner of love the Father hath bestowed upon us, that we should be called the sons of God: therefore the world knoweth us not, because it knew him not" (1st John 3:1).

• Children of God are loved by their heavenly Father. The love He has for His own is not inconsistent or conditional and dependent upon moods, but it is an eternal love. When you open your eyes in the morning and when you close them at night your first and last thoughts should be, "I am accepted by God and am loved by Him with an eternal love." This complete and total love is described in Romans 8:38–39: "For I am persuaded, that neither death, nor life, nor angels, nor principalities, nor powers, nor things present, nor things to come, nor height, nor depth, nor any other creature, shall be able to separate us from the love of God, which is in Christ Jesus our Lord."

• You have a completely new position because you have become a new person. Many people wish that they could start all over again. A new beginning is exactly what you will receive when you put your faith in Him. "Therefore if any man be in Christ, he is a new creature: old things are passed away; behold, all things are become new" (2nd Corinthians 5:17).

• As a child of God, you may now have access to the Father through Jesus Christ: "Be careful for nothing; but in every thing by prayer and supplication with thanksgiving let your requests be made known unto God. And the peace of God, which passeth all understanding, shall keep your hearts and minds through Christ Jesus"(Philippians 4:6–7).

• You may know that you have a God who is faithful and who keeps His promises. The guarantee of your reaching your goal does not lie with you, but with Him. You may trust Him completely in good days and bad. He will not leave you or forsake you: "...being confident of this very thing, that he which hath begun a good work in you will perform it until the day of Jesus Christ" (Philippians 1:6).

• You may have the assurance that every "little," "big," or "grievous" sin from your past has been blotted out if you have sincerely confessed it and asked the Lord for forgiveness. Through this complete forgiveness, you are also liberated from all occult or demonic entanglement. You are no longer under the spell or influence of the devil, but under the lordship of Jesus: "...blotting out the handwriting of ordinances that was against us, which was contrary to us, and took it out of the way, nailing it to his cross; and having spoiled principalities and powers, he made a shew of them openly, triumphing over them in it" (Colossians 2:14–15).

Do not despair when you have fallen into sin after you have become a child of God. Confess your sins to the Lord, ask His forgiveness and repent. "My little children, ᴎese things write I unto you, that ye sin not. And if any man sin, we have an advocate with the Father, Jesus Christ the righteous" (1st John 2:1).

• Your life has been given meaning! Many people will spend their entire lives looking for the meaning of life. The true meaning of life is to know God and His Son, Jesus Christ, to live in fellowship with Him, and to have eternal life, "And we know that the Son of God is come, and hath given us an understanding, that we may know him that is true, and we are in him that is true, even in his Son Jesus Christ. This is the true God, and eternal life" (1st John 5:20).

• You may be assured of eternal salvation: "These things have I written unto you that believe on the name of the Son of God; that ye may know that ye have eternal life, and that ye may believe on the name of the Son of God" (1st John 5:13).

• When you have intimate fellowship with Jesus, you may also know that the Lord gives you the strength to cope with all of the worries of your daily life. You will no longer depend on your own strength and talents, for the Bible says, "He giveth power to the faint; and to them that have no might he increaseth strength" (Isaiah 40:29).

• The Lord also gives peace and joy! The life of a Christian is by no means boring, as some people think. On the contrary, faith in Jesus and practical discipleship make life interesting. We experience God in our daily lives. The Lord has promised us this peace and joy; "Peace I leave with you, my peace I give unto you: not as the world giveth, give I unto you. Let not your heart be troubled, neither let it be afraid" (John 14:27). "These things have I spoken unto you, that my joy might remain in you, and that your joy might be full"(John 14:7). "I am come that they might have life, and that they might have it more abundantly"(John 10:10).

Isn't It Worth It To Be A Christian?

It would be wrong, however, to think that the life of a Christian is a bed of roses and that you will never have any more problems. Actually, the life of a

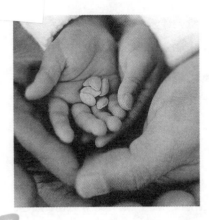

"We know with certainty that our lives are safe in His hands and that He will carry us through various crises."

believer who follows the Lord without compromising can be full of trials and temptations.

Christians are not spared pain, illness, sorrow and misfortune. But hard times become more bearable because we have the assurance that nothing that happens can make God's promises void.

We know with certainty that our lives are safe in His hands and that He will carry us through various crises. We also know that we have a living hope. The knowledge that the hardships a Christian may have to endure are not the end, but the glory that follows gives us strength, peace and security. That is why it pays to be a Christian!

Chapter 7

Jésus: Unique, Incomparable and Wonderful in His Return

*T*he Lord was referring to Himself when He said: "Behold, he cometh with clouds; and every eye shall see him, and they also which pierced him: and all kindreds of the earth shall wail because of him. Even so, Amen. I am Alpha and Omega, the beginning and the ending, saith the Lord, which is, and which was, and which is to come, the Almighty" (Revelation 1:7–8). Psalm 89:6 is prophetically speaking of His return: "For who in the heaven can be compared unto the Lord? Who among the sons of the mighty can be likened unto the Lord?" Jesus will return, at first only for those who believe in Him, to take them to heaven. About seven years later, He will come to this earth visibly in the clouds of glory to judge the world and establish His kingdom. Everything in world history is moving towards His return.

Dr. Theo Lehmann wrote this concerning the future: "Here Christ, the Risen Lord, is speaking. Jesus does not belong to those who are here for a while and then disappear in the fog of history. His name does not belong to those that are in the media for a time and after a few years are forgotten... He is the first, the Creator of this world – and He is the last. When they have all disappeared, the gods and idols, the systems, the philosophies, the mighty builders of great ideologies, of imposing buildings, of oppressing places of exile, when they have all disappeared from the windows of their palaces, when they have toppled from their positions, when they have come down from their high horses and statues, when they have returned to dust – forgotten and forsaken, when this whole world has fallen: Jesus will still be there. The gods and idols of the past and of today, you will never meet again. But you will meet Jesus. He is at the end of history, and also at the end of your life."

Acts 10:42 says: "And he commanded us to preach unto the people, and to testify that it is he which was ordained of God to be the Judge of quick and dead." This means nothing other than that the moment is coming when every person will have to stand before the unique, incomparable and wonderful Lord – some will stand before Him as eternally saved, and those who have rejected His divine offer of salvation will stand before Him eternally lost. That is why you should become a Christian and not resist Him any longer!

Paul tried to resist Jesus, but when the Lord met Paul, we read: "And when we were all fallen to the earth, I heard a voice speaking unto me, and saying in the Hebrew tongue, Saul, Saul, why persecutest thou me? It is hard for thee to kick against the pricks" (Acts 26:14). Bible commentators explain that this is a proverbial expression of the Greeks. The picture is of a stubborn mule that brings greater pain upon itself when it kicks out at the goad of the driver. The meaning of the expression is, "You are trying to resist Me in vain."

Jesus is also unique in that He does not withdraw from sinners; He turns to them. For this reason He came to the earth, died and rose again. He loves you as no other person does, and He is approaching you today in all of His great love. He alone has the power to forgive all of your sins, to receive you into His kingdom and to give you eternal life. Won't you take hold of the hand He is extending to you today?

Jésus: Unique, Incomparable and Wonderful in His Heavenly Reward for His Children

*C*hildren of God will receive a body that is similar to His glorious body.

While we are alive, we live in a mortal body that is subject to sickness, age and ultimately death. Our body is limited and bears the marks of sin. On the day of the Rapture (or the resurrection of the dead, should we die before the Rapture) the Lord will give His children a glorious body: "For our conversation is in heaven; from whence also we look for the Saviour, the Lord Jesus Christ: who shall change our vile body, that it may be fashioned like unto his glorious body, according to the working whereby he is able even to subdue all things unto himself" (Philippians 3:20–21).

We are called "...to the obtaining of the glory of our Lord Jesus Christ" (2nd Thessalonians 2:14). What a great privilege! What an honor! Our bodies will be like His glorious body. That does not mean that we will be like the Lord in His divinity, but we will resemble Him. We will look different, but we will still be recognizable as individuals. This new body will no longer be subject to decay, but will be suited to the conditions of heaven.

Children Of God Will Be Heirs Of God

Ephesians 1:18 says that we will be heirs of God: "...the eyes of your understanding being enlightened; that ye may know what is the hope of his calling, and what the riches of the glory of his inheritance in the saints." Believers in Christ will be revealed in the eternal heavens before the angels of God as sons and daughters of the heavenly Father. As children of God, we will be heirs to the riches of God's glory. This surpasses all of the powers of imagination. There can be nothing greater.

If you have received Jesus into your heart and are following Him, you will take part in all that God is and all that belongs to Him. In other words, you will take part in all of heaven's glory.

To be God's heir means to lack nothing. Everything will be in abundance and unimaginably beautiful in heaven. The Bible contains an awesome description of heaven in Revelation 21 and 22:

• The building material of the walls of the heavenly Jerusalem will be jasper.

• The city and its streets will be of gold, like glass. We cannot even imagine this type of splendor.

• The walls' foundations will be embellished with the finest precious stones and the twelve doors of the entrance into the city will consist of twelve pearls that are as large as the city gate.

• From the throne of God and the Lamb will proceed a river of the water of life, sparkling like crystal.

Someone once said this concerning the glory of heaven, "We do not pay anything, but we experience everything – not a minute or an hour but a whole eternity." Why? Because Jesus paid the entire price for our salvation. He paid for our entrance into heaven with His blood (Hebrews 10:19–20).

Children Of God Will Live With God And Jesus Christ

The Lord Jesus Himself promised us this when He said, "In my Father's house are many mansions...I go to prepare a place for you. And if I go and prepare a place for you, I will come again, and receive you unto myself; that where I am, there ye may be also" (John 14:2–3). One day, we will live with God. All human powers of imagination are not powerful enough to comprehend the glory of the Father's house. What we may know, however, is the following:

• God Himself is the architect of this house. According to Hebrews 11:10, He is the "builder and maker" of this eternal dwelling place.

81

• These houses are incomparably beautiful because they are not made by the hands of men, but built through the power of God (2nd Corinthians 5:1).

• This heavenly dwelling place does not need any natural or artificial light. It does not depend on the sun or the moon because God's glory illuminates it with the light of the Lamb of God, the Lord Jesus Christ (Revelation 21:23).

• There will be more than enough room in this heavenly home for every believer in Jesus Christ from all times and all nations.

• Children of God will celebrate an eternal feast in fellowship with God the Father and the Lord Jesus Christ.

We read about this unimaginably beautiful feast in Revelation 21:3: "And I heard a great voice out of heaven saying, Behold, the tabernacle of God is with men, and he will dwell with them, and they shall be his people, and God himself shall be with them, and be their God." Heaven is a place of unspeakable joy and perfect happiness because God dwells in the midst of His people. Not one single negative aspect of this world will be present there (Revelation 21:27).

Heaven is compared to a wedding, the greatest of all celebrations.

John 16:20,22 and 24 says that all sorrow will be turned into joy and that this perfect joy will never be taken away from us.

Peter wrote, "Jesus Christ...whom having not seen, ye love; in whom, though now ye see him not, yet believing, ye rejoice with joy unspeakable and full of glory" (1st Peter 1:8).

In light of this, we are also able to understand Jesus' words, "Rejoice, because your names are written in heaven" (Luke 10:20).

Our senses will also be filled with delight; this is how I understand the words of 1st Corinthians 2:9, "But as it is written (in Isaiah 64:3), Eye hath not seen, nor ear heard, neither have entered into the heart of man, the things which God hath prepared for them that love him."

Heaven will be full of life! There will be no lack of anything, for nothing can be added to it or improved upon. Boredom will be unknown because heaven is perfect and infinite; it is the perfection of a full life.

Children Of God Will Have No More Unanswered Questions In Heaven

Every question will be answered and every "why?" will be silenced. We will see and understand everything in the light of Jesus. Not even the slightest trace of doubt will remain. The Lord Jesus says this so comfortingly: "And ye now therefore have sorrow: but I will see you again, and your heart shall rejoice, and your joy no man taketh from you. And in that day ye shall ask me nothing" (John 16:22–23). We will suddenly understand that all things worked together for our good.

Children Of God Are At The Coronation And Reign In Heaven

Everything that we, as children of God who are saved by grace, do in this life in the name of the Lord Jesus will retain an eternal dimension. Thus, the crown of righteousness is promised to all those who love His appearing (2nd Timothy 4:7-8). The Bible also speaks of an incorruptible crown (1st Corinthians 9:25), of a crown of glory (1st Peter 5:4), and a crown of life (James 1:12).

In the book of Daniel, we read that those who turn many to righteousness and participated in the spread of the Gospel will shine like the stars forever and ever (Daniel 12:3). And the Lord Jesus said, "Then shall the righteous shine forth as the sun in the kingdom of their Father" (Matthew 13:43). The Holy Scriptures relate that those who belong to the Lord will rule with Him forever and ever (Revelation 22:5).

Children Of God Are In A Place Of Perfect Love In Heaven

First Corinthians 13:8, 13 says that love will never cease. In heaven, we will live in direct fellowship with the One who is love, who incorporates love with His whole being. Hatred and other such negative things are completely unknown in heaven. Love alone will rule and everyone will be loved by everyone.

Heaven Is Also A Place Where Many Things Will No Longer Exist

Revelation 21:4 promises that there will be no more tears in heaven (Revelation 21:4).

There will be no more dreams. Our lives on earth are comprised of dreams and fantasies. We dream about the ideal job, the best vacation, the perfect partner and the most romantic wedding. All of these dreams and longings will end because the reality and glory of heaven will surpass them.

There will be no more sea (Revelation 21:1). The sea is always a picture of restlessness; restlessness of the nations as well as the restlessness, of our own hearts and those of a demonized humanity. In heaven, everything will come to rest and eternal peace will reign.

There will be no more sorrow, weeping, pain or fear in heaven (Revelation 21:4). There will be no more curse (Revelation 22:3), no more night (Revelation 22:5), and death will be abolished (Revelation 20:14 and 21:4).

Nothing will be as it was. God will make all things new, completely new! Moreover, in heaven there will be things we've never seen or experienced before (Revelation 21:4–5).

We cannot be driven out of heaven because it is the final dwelling place for those who believe in Jesus. The splendor of heaven will be experienced for eternity, for we are born again,"...to an inheritance incorruptible, and undefiled, and that fadeth not away, reserved in heaven for you" (1st Peter 1:4).

There will be no sin in heaven. That is why nobody with sin can enter into heaven: "And there shall in no wise enter into it any thing that defileth, neither whatsoever worketh abomination, or maketh a lie: but they which are written in the Lamb's book of life" (Revelation 21:27, compare also with verse 8).

Just as heaven is a wonderful reality, hell, in contrast, is a terrible reality. Jesus spoke of hell very often. Hell is where all that eternal glory which we tried to describe with our inadequate words will not be. It is a place of eternal separation from God and that which He has promised to Jesus' disciples. Hell is a place of torment for those who have not received forgiveness of their sins through the blood of the Lamb of God.

Jesus Christ is the only Redeemer who suffered for us in order to attain and guarantee our entrance into heaven. Only those who believe in Jesus and surrender their lives to Him and lay their guilt and sins at His feet will gain entrance into the kingdom of God.

Somebody once asked, "Why in the world do we flee from life, when we fear death? Why do we flee from the truth, when we are afraid of lies? Why do we remain on our crooked path, when the path of sin brings us to perdition? Jesus Christ is the way, the truth and the life. Those who are against Jesus have no future. Yet everyone longs for life. That is the way we are made. The last part of the journey seals our eternal damnation without Jesus. Yet people who are led by Jesus Christ have a glorious future. Their Lord is returning! In faith they see a new heaven and a new earth!"

I will say it again: It really pays to be a Christian!

Chapter 9

How You
Can Become
A Christian Today

Turn to the Lord in prayer. Tell Him that you want to believe in Him, and ask Him to forgive your sins.

Invite Him into your life. Tell Him that you want Him to be your Lord and Master and that you want Him to take over the leadership of your life for the rest of your life.

Thank the Lord Jesus Christ for dying on the cross for you and your sins: Thank Him for rising from the dead in order to give you eternal life. John 1:12 says, "As many as received him, to them gave he power to become the sons of God, even to them that believe on his name."

Share your faith with others. Read the Bible daily and seek fellowship with those who also believe in Jesus.

If you have any questions about salvation, please write to us at:

Midnight Call Ministries
P.O.BOX 280008
Columbia, SC 29228

REPLY FORM

❏ I believe that God was speaking to me through the pages of this booklet and have decided to follow Jesus and to ask Him into my life this day of _____.

Name: _____

Address: _____

City: _____ St: _____

Zip: _____ Country: _____

⏭ *Tap into the Bible analysis of top prophecy authorities...*

Midnight Call is a hard-hitting Bible-based magazine loaded with news, commentary, special features, and teaching, illustrated with explosive color pictures and graphics. Join hundreds of thousands of readers in 140 countries who enjoy this magazine regularly!

⏭ *The world's leading prophetic Bible magazine*

⏭ *Covering international topics with detailed commentary*

⏭ *Bold, uncompromising biblical stands on issues*

⏭ *Pro-Bible, pro-family, pro-life*

12 issues/1 yr. $28.95
24 issues/2 yr. $45

Mail with payment to: Midnight Call • P.O. Box 280008 • Columbia, SC 29228 1054

❑ YES! I would like to subscribe to *Midnight Call* magazine!
   ❑ 12 issues/1 yr. $28⁹⁵   ❑ 24 issues/2 yr. $45
     ❑ Cash ❑ Check ❑ Master/Visa/Discover
     With Credit Card, you may also dial toll-free, 1–800–845–2420

Card#_____ Exp:_____

Name:_____

Address:_____

City:_____ St:_____ Zip:_____

Book Resources

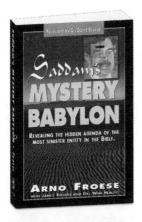

SADDAM'S MYSTERY BABYLON

Item # 1034 • Pages 272–Paperback • Price $11.99

The Old Testament book of Daniel identifies the four Gentile superpowers as Babylon, Medo-Persia, Greece and Rome. All nations, regardless of prestige, wealth or size fall into one of these categories. *Saddam's Mystery Babylon* offers convincing evidence over a much-confused issue: The Old Testament's ancient Babylon and the "Mystery Babylon" of the book of Revelation are two very separate, unique and distinct entities. The author outlines the qualifications which reveal an unmasked "Mystery Babylon."

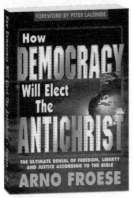

HOW DEMOCRACY WILL ELECT THE ANTICHRIST

Item # 1033 • Pages 288–Paperback • Price $11.99

British statesman, Winston Churchill said, "Democracy is the worst form of government, but it is the best we have." Why did Churchill make such a negative comment about a system lauded and approved by people all over the world? Isn't the method of electing your own government officials considered to be the ultimate freedom? *How Democracy Will Elect The Antichrist* offers clear revelation illustrating that we have, in fact, reached the end stages of the end-times, and that a peaceful system such as democracy will install the Antichrist!

TERROR OVER AMERICA

Item # 1050 • Pages 128–Paperback • Price $9.99

This book goes beyond the September 11th atrocities and reveals several reasons for the great conflict between Christianity, Islam, and the tiny country in between — Israel. The book also contains an explanation of how this act of terror against the United States fits into this development, and what it means to believers.